Blossoming

Blossoming

Alishia McCullough

Blossoming is an exploration of mental health, self-love, and healing, as the author takes the reader on a journey towards self-discovery and acceptance.

This book is for those struggling to accept themselves or struggling with relationships or societal expectations. Each chapter evolves, like the development of a butterfly, allowing the reader to embark on a journey of growth.

This is for my blood family and chosen family, who encourage me to access my potential and foster my resilience and confidence. Thank you for always reminding me that life has many turns; however, it will always lead to a destination. To Katie, for opening numerous of possibilities with your wisdom, insight, patience, and hope. To Miesha, for all of your support, time, and feedback.

Contents

Blossoming is cyclical: an ever-changing evolution of life. My journey is never-ending, and my perspective is always changing, like the stages of the butterfly. Each stage holds its own beauty as part of the process of creating a unique and beautiful creature. The process is essential to the development of wings that allow one to break through societal expectations and self-doubt, becoming their true authentic self.

Chapter 1: Egg

"Seasons"

Inhaling--

your presence retrievable,

tiny crinkles in the corners of your eyes,

golden brown leaves crunching softly beneath our feet,

a chill shaking my body,

your arms quickly blanketing me,

the ferris wheel

blurring out the world as we rock slowly,

my heart transient

in a mirror of endless stars,

the closest to heaven I will ever be,

the night calls closing time,

below the carousel spins monotonously,

shy giggles ring in my ears,

you are safety

your heart beats in this floppy tune,

I exhale--

as the moment becomes stuck in time

"I Am Sorry"

head buried in my right hand

ink creating nonsense on a blue lined distressed sheet

3 missed calls and 2 years later--- late

hinges and frame shaking as you made your final statement

my distant stare pleading for the forgiveness of the white door

and apologies in the shaken window frame

while searching for inspiration behind the glass

that's the problem

I am always searching for something else

my finger nails attacked by ruminations

I crumple the paper

"Letting a Beast off the Leash"

the past few minutes blotted out

and now I'm in this icky and sticky place

it feels like fire and hot sauce

pounding in my chest

organs swelling and ribs cracking

my stomach boiling with something red and dark blue

vomiting out a string of the most unforgivable

turning to my awful muse

high on the fumes

empty as they begin to settle

my amygdala overwhelmed

unconsciousness is my only escape

those sneaky bastard of emotions

"Archaic Junk in my Attic"

we live on forever in your mom's antique picture frame

passion steadily melting like snow crystals

transforming with every camera flash

blinded by the present, unaware of the future

memories escaping us like grains of sand

as we find new place holders to occupy the empty space

"Addiction"

social acceptability

your friends think you are the shit girl

void of everything imperfect

always putting on a show

and they clap and laugh

encouraging you to do what "cool girls" do

your tough exterior invincible to pain---

until the party is over and you are forced to be alone

realizing choices and consequences are closely related

you are fighting with the strength inside of you

but relapse is a frequent visitor

knocking on your front door

and you are trying to avoid the unwanted company

hiding your trauma and pain in the dusty attic

and shutting your insecurities behind locked doors

while forcing down the happy pill to keep up the façade

"Another 4 AM Conversation"

your words suffocating me,

venom running deep, like the cuts across my wrist

my breath becoming shallow as you continue to speak

you wear your secrets in the same place I wear my heart

poker face has never been your expertise

in my deepest valley

your presence is dust

unbeknownst to you, the relationship died long ago

I've been retreating into my mind with rhetorical questions

fading into the grey matter

and masking my sadness as I smile and say "it's okay, baby"

"Romantic Getaways to the Cabin"

flames are the little things that make the fire

I see an array of red and orange as the stakes become higher

these flames have become ritualistic

as he apologizes and promises it won't happen again

glass cuts into the soles of my feet

his bloody fist paints my face

he and Jack Daniels enjoy this game

he stumbles through the chaos to find the darts

while flames pierce the chambers that protect my heart

I am burning, drenched in gasoline

he smirks while soothing his rage in my pain

and my voice disappears in the crackling warmth of the flames

"Long Empty nights"

the weight of loneliness

blankets me like a thick morning fog

leaving me with this unescapable dewiness

rivers of sadness flow from my body

I am lost.

disconnected from the present moment

my thoughts become thin threads, holding on to

remnants of desire for the love I wanted most

haunting me, in this rickety town of mine

a reminder that as I am making strides forward

my frame always shifts

placing me behind this thick and muffling glass

I scream

"A Beautiful Storm"

my mind is twisted like an unkempt garden

it's too late to save me, and my heart has hardened

the thorns stick into my spine

keeping me in this hunched over position

eyes learning the patterns in the sidewalks

no one really knows me...

a hurricane destroying everything that it finds

leaving behind a sky of faint colorful lines

but all we remember is the storm

"You Thought You Were Chris Brown"

my chest left bare, where your head used to rest

the boundaries of my universe are kaleidoscopic

we climbed a mountain and only one of us returned

tears decorate my pillow

sacrifices on a predestined script

my flimsy heart was your stage

and we were casted as Satan and Eve

sweet indulgence tempted my innocent desire

time extended into extremities

as I took my first bite into heartbreak

"Haunted"

the ghost of our love travels on the tracks

it gently whispers memories back

empty heartbeats from the chest of my pillow

provide the only comfort I have for tonight

I wear my insecurities like an anchor around my neck

drowning ---

loneliness is flowing from my body

I'm always on the edge of pressing send

before my pride pulls me back to safety

shadows of "should haves" dance upon these ivory walls

"The Existentialism of Our Relationship"

standing on the corner I watch the cars go by

I'm on the edge with tears in my eyes

you stand in the warmth embedded in her smile

wrapped up in the comfort of your lies

aching inside, snowflakes grace my lips

the world is passing by so fast

I close my eyes as thoughts of you become transient

headlights illuminate the snow

spasms flow through my body like music

my fingers entangle with the delicate frost

the flatbed, smooth and steady, crystallizes my thoughts

my lids relax, and I exhale peace

taking the first step at the horn of an angel's trumpet

blaring through the night as if to welcome me home

enclosed by the psychedelic hues of grey

as I begin to drift into the antimatter

"The Cycle of Life"

he is the skeleton that sits at the front of the room

slowly decaying

always present and absent

his bangs growing like tree roots

the hour glass holding his porcelain soul quickly growing tired

a small laugh constantly begging for salvation as he curls his lips

his eyes have seen death and life

a tear slides down his cheek

as he whispers for salvation into the ears of demons

"They Always Come Back"

twisting like vines

tangled in the stories that continue to grow

each one flutters from his lips

the knots in my stomach continue to tighten

making it impossible to breathe

nightmares began to paint my reality

my patience is worn like old batteries

you are not the first impression

curtains rise, lights fill the set

I watch you stumble around with a blank stare

I am your only audience

you only know how to pretend while I get lost in my mind

the lights go down on the scene

the show is over bringing you down to one knee

lips quivering and pleading out

for flowers in the garden that you left to die

"Pilot" Episode 1

I outran the shadows

escaped from that grey cloud

cremated the sorrow

and sent it down the kitchen sink

washed my hands clean

no more pain to make numb

I've dyed my hair and changed my number

budding flowers take away the blues

fresh showers wash away the damage

birds are migrating towards paradise

and I am ready for flight

Chapter 2: Larva

"Forgiveness"

as I turn the page, I am granted new eyes

my heart spinning on a loom

repeatedly healing itself

stitch after stich

spinning together this tapestry of my life

tears cascade down my cheeks

drip... drip... drip

the steel roof has a leek

soaking the untouchable parts of me

bringing down the wall twice my size

and finally looking at you, with a new set of eyes

"Silence this loud"

your silence screams into a rainy Sunday afternoon

I have the answers, yet your voice left unheard

a harsh wind whispers my forthcoming fate

as I cower into my seat of denial

confusion and assumptions toy with my mind

a straight arrow separates us

the wall is rebuilt with fresh cement

this silence divides us more and more

we both know the end, but won't utter the words

that are yelling in the silence, but to us, left unheard

"Smell the Roses"

our lives are like glass in the hands of
children

in this world as visitors to liberty

looking back and saying "where has
the time gone"

looking forward and praying for
more

ignorant to our time piece

our drinks and pills, close allies

shortening the gap between her
screams of agony

and their heavy hearts as the casket
sinks into the ground

extracting memories like a soul
leaving bones and flesh

as the dirt pulls us into an eternal
embrace

"The End of the Summer"

disbelief left on the edge of my shallow breath

I am looking in a rear-view mirror

my mind yelling "GO"!

my heart pleading "stay"

while you hold my world in the hazel of your eyes

silently begging for forgiveness

as you always do...

bruises mark your neck

daring me to ask, "who is she?"

159.7 miles and a day later

would have saved you

"I love you"

has become an excuse to do as you please

"My Favorite Season"

cool nights, autumn leaves

changing colors, swaying trees

jackets, boots, and football games

summer love washed away in the rain

the views from the fair, overlooking the crowd

the world moves on as we spin around

we celebrate the homecoming king and queen

and then get dressed up for Halloween

sunsets go down and the parties begin

tipsy at tailgates, hoping the night will never end

"Puppeteer"

a round of applause for the puppeteer

he is perfect at stringing hearts

a desperate cry, a fallen tear

and his charm will warm your heart

with every word he lures you in

letting you fall in an imaginary net

signing your blinded love

to be an actor on his set

suddenly, he's got you strung you're his new conundrum

caught in his alluring mirage

he has your heart on the strings

now he can unmask the façade

"Lust"

he'd say,

come on over, give it up, it's just a little pussy

and there I'd come, leaving him satisfied

but I'd feel like a little pussy

I could say no

but I tend to believe in sparks that never ignite

he strokes his ego as I slide into Victoria's Secret's latest special

caught in the washing machine of his careless ways

desperate to leave, but yearning for him to see galaxies in my soul

he would always half smile and expect me when the stars came out

sticking around to play with the dark curls in his hair

praying the daylight would bring an awakening

to the "man" trapped in the boy

I was quickly approaching an expiration

my self-esteem wallowing in the expectations

of a human who only knew my silhouette

I was tired of being just a little pussy

"Sex"

sex without vulnerability

is the emptiness we feel when we fake satisfaction

it's the failure we experience from pleasing everyone except ourselves

it's the meaning we search for in the wrinkled sheets

and the insecurities in our flaws

as we focus on faking a Grammy winning climax

the longing to reach ecstasy without authenticity

as we continue to look for someone to make us feel wanted

to make us feel sexy, youthful, attractive, and desirable

rough hands holding the love handles we never learned to love

we won't let go of perfection, out of fear

that freedom exposes the naked person we neglect in the mirror

as we shame ourselves for who we really are

who are you? who is he? who is she? who are they?

sex without vulnerability is disconnection

"You Could Make the World Stop with Your Tongue"

music brings people together

but the end of the verse drifts them apart

the nights that left our faces tilted upwards

yelling through the sunroof on the ride home

the night when I first heard the guitar

calling out to me through my darkness

a sweet melancholic voice, softly singing along to Tracy Chapman

our eyes meet, revealing nothing

and the song ends, while the last chord echoes in the silence

"The Good Teen and the Problems with Perfectionism"

went to church every week

only to sneak out the back door when no one was watching

I had a great job for my age

but I would steal for the thrill of feeling something

something I was missing

always bringing home good grades, no trouble at school

weekends spent with whatever suitable lover at the time

and my partner in crime

designing my body with ink on an apartment mattress

wild and tipsy nights, morning sun caressing our faces

but I was still alone

still depressed

trying to find safety in a broken teenage boy

my parents never knew and never thought to ask

because I was a good teen,

cutting away the pain, earning academic awards

always smiling and faking that I was okay

"The American Dream"

awake and asleep

I have the same dream

it's always unreachable, but vividly seen

I am not alone in this race for identity

each person is running and dreaming simultaneously

the dream masks the faces of mobility and stagnation

some selling their souls to reach that white picket fence

but the dream is not always as attainable as it seems to be

yet, we swear we are better off in this race

unaware that our minds are creating an imaginary place

"Rolling Stones"

you told me to keep the car running

even though the radio doesn't play our songs

what we had was Jimi Hendrix and Janis Joplin

that Coachella type of shit

I loved you with acid eyes

on a high, steadily heading for an abrupt ending

psychedelic colors invade my mind

leaving me in the middle of the festival

dancing alone

"Day Dreaming"

today I saw a bird

he was hanging in a tree

even uncaged, he wasn't free

I still see your face

sometimes it visits my dreams

I still hear that guitar

making out the sounds of Fast Car

a little piece is holding on

hoping that you are coming home

although I know your heart is gone

I am wishing for one more song

"To the 'FuckBoys'

she is not a container

to dump your unprocessed emotional baggage

she is not a placeholder

for the girl who broke your heart

you do not get to tell her that you love her

when you have no intention of properly loving her

you do not have the right to play jack in the box

in her life

your inferiority complex is not an excuse to make her feel small

and denial is not a courtesy to extend dishonesty

your inability to love and respect yourself

should not be displaced on her

"Cocaine"

days turn to months

and I wonder if I ever cross your mind

all those empty "could have's"

your broken soul

escaping the confines of healing

the seasons have changed

and I am just another captured milestone

I noticed,

when someone cares for you

you shut down

and I know you loved before

but she betrayed you

and now you say the world is cold

please fix your heart

because I cannot try anymore

while you hurt her through me

as the memories fade

because I loved the potential of a man

that I never met, while you buried us

in the comfort of those white lines

"White Supremacy"

you have drawn the line

picked apart our differences

and called it biology

you kill our spirit

you ignore the trauma

and continue to hold us down

I was born with a boulder on my shoulders

and you stand on it, pushing me into the ground

we pray for peace and love

but you literally take the breath from our lips

behind every criminalized media story

you destroy an empire of Kings and Queens

we live in a world without protection

because you hold all the power

a family grieves, and seconds turn to hours

no amount of education can change

what has been done or what is to come

change is hope suffocated, before it leaves the tongue

we live in generational struggle

but you have peace of mind

while we aim for survival, anxiety etched into our DNA

while you attempt to brainwash us by whiting out history

"Astrological Lovers"

the end

tearing apart the sun and the moon

together, their force could be powerful

but fate destroys the nature of their greatness

the sun falls into the flames

the darkness holds the moon in paralysis

keeping them from coexisting together

while communicating through the zodiac

of pairs that were never compatible

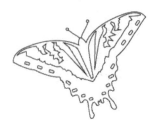

Chapter 3: Pupa

"Just Us"

same man, different face

different story, same ending

he smiles and builds up my hopes

with empty promises

I cannot do this again

but it is the only thing that I know

I always plan to leave

but I am convinced to stay

through a broken image of change

same lust, different body

different words, same meaning

he just takes until I have nothing left

"Just Me"

a tainted smile is all I have left

after all, you took everything else

"us" fading away as the days crawl by

I trust in people who let me down

an empty bottle is my only consistency

helping me erase my memories until you are gone

but it doesn't keep me from feeling alone

so, I search for something to fill your place

but that doesn't heal me

it is the same ending different face

and now pain is all I have left.

"Slipping down the Spiral Staircase"

I'm fresh out,

out of energy to keep spilling the ink

on the same ending of a story

too tired of getting close to happiness

but having it disappear like a mirage

grasping for love as it disintegrates

like cyclical clock work

burning a hole in my heart, mind, and soul

leaving poisoned fumes

I'm so trusting...

in a boy with a broken image of himself

the boy who is in battle with his identity

that I have already lost

feeling as if I will never be enough

the faster I run

the further the finish line seems to be

these poisoned fumes cloud my vision

and I cannot see

"Silly Me"

the fear of being alone

a feeling so strong

that even the simplest person

can turn into someone you would not

spend a day without

avoidance of the truth

an action so strong

that you prolong the time you should be

letting him go

telling yourself that good will come

where only dead ends are in sight

turning your "I would never"

into "I'll do anything" just don't

leave me alone

"Blank Mind, Colorful Heart"

I'm so glad

I was shown the light

in the darkest pit of my life

I'm so grateful that the pain eating away

at my mind and body

has been beaten

I am blessed that I can stand up

and raise my fist as a symbol of pride and power

for all the power he has granted us

I am thankful that he has opened my eyes

to reveal that I was putting trust in faux safety

my God, you can turn a mess into a miracle

I am grateful that every day you show me

that you brought me too far to leave me

I pray that you continue to order my steps

because you allowed man to walk on water

therefore, I am fearless!

your love is limitless, and your grace is plenty

and you have giving me unmerited favor

"Society"

my thoughts race with the images of black men on the news

filtered through perceptions of criminalization

skin hue their only weapon

their bodies designed with bullet holes

a family accepts a future of struggle and pain

burying their dreams in unforgiving soil

childhoods robbed as black and brown kids understand their harsh realities

school systems decide that they are not enough

the government determines they are not enough

fighting institutions in a stacked and unfair game

prisons are the slavery of the 21st century

black women are treated more like property than a "family house dog"

pain and struggles are invalidated because "that happened 400 years ago"

the systems are broken, what family wealth?

we cannot talk about mental health, understandably we don't trust the medical field

how can I make my mark on society?

when it permanently stamped me sooner than I was conceived

how can I be at peace in my society?

when society has already taken every piece of me

"Depression"

all my life, I've had dreams

that my fate would depend

on how fast I was able to run

there was something chasing me that seemed impossible to escape

each dream I'd run faster and faster

almost getting away, but missing the opportunity

the harder I tried

the less I seemed to be moving

I could see the destination

but as I am running my legs become weak

and I am fighting to win

yet I cannot go much farther before that dark cloud catches up

and I am consumed

"Therapy"

Inviting

dark space

filled by a heavy thick and dusty book

titled "My Past"

luring me to discover the unknown

to understand, to heal

to free my mind

"Isolation"

thoughts take over

like the sound of a bee in my ear

I can't escape them once they begin

they bring worry,

then the buzzing starts

and I am too exhausted to reach out

to share my experiences

with the ears of brick walls

"Growing into a Woman"

I hold my breath

and look in the mirror

my heart drops

and the feeling of defeat takes over

I strip down bare

and step on the scale

I feel disgusted

and my body feels heavy

I refuse to wear clothes that I like

because they reveal those insecurities

my mother sees herself when she looks at me

she says, "don't put that on" and feels relief

when she notices my weight loss

oblivious to the many meals my body went without

to fit the picture that society captured...

and then distorted,

until it was framed into a photo

that society accepted as "beauty"

I have never been a conformist

however, it's impossible to escape the expectations

and slowly the messages, seep into my mind

telling me not to eat this and that

"work out more, eat less"

and I internalize those voices

until the growing woman begins to shrink

"You Knew Me Before I Knew Myself"

years later, I can live in that moment

when life is hard,

when a certain song reminds me of that feeling

I go there,

I go back to her, a youthful and optimistic me

in limbo about a big life decision, but still grounded

still aware of the moment she created with you

she lays on your tan chest

time is running out

but she does this for me...

for her future. Her eyes memorize your face

every freckle, every smile line, every flaw

and those eyes...

she loses herself in you,

holding on in vulnerability, in that happiness

knowing it was only temporary

but forever a memory,

forever a moment

"We Wear Our Body Art Like Battle Wounds"

sometimes I wonder if anything ever changes

I feel like I am living in an alternate universe

moving and growing consciously

but unconsciously knowing I belong somewhere else

somewhere with you

"Growth"

growth is this result that everyone notices

as they congratulate you and acknowledge your accolades

growth is the unseen process

that seems to move like molasses

slowing seeping into every vein

and mixing with my genetics

at some point I don't recognize myself

the past is seen from different eyes

a new mind, a new perspective

and I stand on the stage as the curtain rises

the crowd is cheering, their faces filled with joy

I feel good, I finally made it!

and... I feel alone,

this crowd witnessing my beginning and end

but missing

my struggles, my pain, my restless nights

my small successes, my heartbreaks

my let downs and my barriers

my empty bottles before bed and roasted coffee by morning

all to stand here on display as the product

an epitome of success

unrecognizable to myself, but all so familiar

I smile, I wave, I bow...

the cameras flash

"Closure"

I am drifting

further away

out of mind, out of space

fading into nothing

I have been waiting for your return

your acknowledgement

your burning desire

but you boarded the bus years ago

never to return,

and I waited at the bus stop

eager every time the door opened

and let down every time it closed

and I sat there alone, with myself

refusing to love

to be love

what is love? I'll wait

I am a ghost, out of your mind

forgotten like childhood memories

simply dust in an empty town

stuck in your past

you have moved on

becoming the man, I envisioned you to be

we planted the seeds

that she waters now as you grow

and all those roots I pulled

all that effort slipping your mind

as you blossom, uproot, and move on

"Smile on His Dimpled Cheeks"

he taught me how to roll out of bed

leaving nothing behind

closing the door on the night before

because that's how this works

I love him in his lows

and he only loves me when I'm high

"Circumstance and Faith are Mostly in Opposition"

it doesn't matter

where I am

all I have to hear is an acoustic guitar

supporting a soft, low voice

a voice tainted by pain and regret

and it's too late

I'm tuned in

listening for something

searching for that feeling

trying to connect

hoping that as I listen

somewhere, you are, too

it's like that thing I told you

go outside, look at the stars

and know that somewhere far away

I am with you

watching and waiting

tune into this

connect with me

"Crawling Out of Dark Years"

thank you,

for trying to love me

for seeing me for the woman I was to become

you always protected me

wiser and more mature

I wasn't ready for that type of commitment

and I pulled away

I was afraid that I deserved better

I got caught up in the cycle, my familiar addiction

and I left

"Just Talking"

fuck boys will be like:

I just want to be friends

but I want you to have sex with me

be emotional and mentally available when I need you

but don't catch feelings because I am not looking for anything serious

and then you will distance yourself

to avoid catching feelings

and you will treat them as if they are just a friend

then they will say, "you changed"

"why are you acting so different?"

"Insight-Awareness"

I have always been afraid

that if I told my true feelings

they would not be reciprocated

and I would be left to clean up

the pieces of rejection

which would be internalized as failure

without defense mechanisms to fall back on

"Holding My Breath under Water Until I Am Forced to Come Up for Air"

cheers to the guy that walked into my life

created a storm and left me to repair the damage

who drained my energy and left me like a dying battery

taking the hands of time and twisting them

months, days, and minutes all wasted

you said you love me,

while still struggling to love yourself

slow to open because your past abused you

everyone left you, and now all you do is leave

you have created this narrative

that has convinced you that no one really cares

you don't trust easily, and commitment is like

nails on a chalkboard, that loud screeching

in your ear, telling you that if you give your all

you will only get hurt

you pushed me away

saying you needed me, but not relying on me enough

saying that I was your all, but finding all in everyone else

leaving me questioning and collecting your pieces

trying to put together a picture that only made sense to you

you never found your purpose, so you follow behind others

you cover up your pride through silence

you hid your insecurities in distance

I finally had to come up for air

left alone to drown

you couldn't even stick around to see the wreck that you made

fear haunts your soul

you only know abandonment

"Apple of My Eye"

looking into the world

I saw a little light

giving me hope in humanity

providing me with a sense of security

bound by a foundation of love and truth

and now destroyed by lies

by betrayal, by fear

openly wounded, yet somehow unharmed

your mysterious aura gave me a sense of peace

as my untold thoughts racing through the back of my mind

finally became evident, a true reality, unveiling my eyes

and pulling me out of the image

far enough for me to see the full picture

now when I look at the world

I see it for what it is

"Slipping"

together, but so far apart

I sense you everywhere

but your presence is absent

so distant, so far, so removed

it is silent

it is still

and I can't find you

"The Receipts"

every time you walk away without looking back

your failure to commit slaps me across the face

wait, no--- it punches me in my stomach

so hard that I still feel impact of the hit months later

you don't talk about anything because it's "not that deep"

fun outings and fancy dinners are your apologies

topped off with sweet nothings and sweaty sheets

and then days turn into weeks,

not a text, not a call, not a visit

my presence doesn't grace the synapses of your mind

you say you love me, but you don't want to be *in* love

you say I'm the "girl" for you, but relationships are too complicated

the funny thing is your inability to give yourself has only extended to me

because she showed me all the messages

and I've read all the receipts

"The Burden of a Guilty Soul"

you sincerely believe you are a good guy

self-awareness has never suited you well

I was the confirmation to your narrative

feeding your ego with that constant validation

when you see me

you refuse to look me directly in the eye

but what are you afraid of?

I see that sheepish look in your insecurity

I hear the guilt in your small talk

I see you pulling away before I even part my lips

your eyes become distant and you get this silly half smile

I see the insincerity and bullshit in every complement

the greed and longing every time you size me up

you stick out your chest thinking you've fooled me again

"Wounds Don't Heal by Adding Salt"

as a society we must stop letting our outer appearances

influence how we interact with and perceive others

we must be aware of our biases, stereotypes, and ism's

we must fight the construct society has fed us from birth

and finally connect with our shared humanity and love for others

we must be aware so that we can come together as one

"A Woman in Society"

when I was about 10 years old, a well-intentioned adult made a comment

towards my body

it still sticks with me to this day,

"you need to watch what you eat"

current statistics run through my head as I remember this encounter

my heart goes out to the 40-60% of girls forced on diets and internalizing

these messages

comparison turns into self-doubt

which turns into an effort to change into an ideal

which may turn into an eating disorder or negative body image

which turns into shame, guilt and loss of control over being aware of your body

until you don't know who you are because the calorie counting

and the weigh-ins

and the internet "body goals" have taken over and we have become so obsessed

but people don't think about this when they make these comments

back then, I wanted to hide my body and shrink

years went on and these messages continued to flood my mind,

"fat is bad", "eat less, work out more"

restriction became a form of control

every magazine in the stores seemed to glorify weight stigma

they said, "skinny is good"

I would get up and work out before I thought to nourish my body

it was routine, and then I got to college

I was finally surrounded by a variety of food options

much like a child starved for years my body craved nourishment

I started to eat unapologetically, I found fun ways to work out

mentally, emotionally, spiritually, and physically I felt better

I was healthy!

and over time the weight picked up

and the disappointed and warning looks became personal

everyone was warning me that I needed to slow down

others would say "the weight looks good on you"

all the messages, all these opinions! I became self-conscious

the old cycle began to creep up and before long I didn't have enough

mental energy to focus

dieting caused me to lose weight, gain it back and lose it again only to feel the shame and disappointment of failure

I tried everything, and I felt as if my body had betrayed me

society had told me that I was undesirable

that a number on the scale defined me as a person

I had to find a redemption---there had to be a way out

and then I found my body salvation

I went through a journey of self-acceptance, discovery,

and body peace and positivity

I was able to define who I was, my strength, my pain, and my worth

I was able to reframe my story and increase my self-esteem

I began setting boundaries and finding balance

I took an active role in advocating for body diversity

the journey has not been a straight perfect path

but like me I hope you find body acceptance and love

"A Woman in Society 2"

welcome to the teenage years,

a time when puberty is rapidly taking over

most people are hormonal and trying to figure out who they are

young girls are sexualized, objectified, mortified, and de-humanized

these were the years when I learned that to be a female in society

meant that I was perceived as less than others

I was socialized to believe that I had less influence and intellect than my male counterparts

these were the years I realized that boys could touch me and get away with it

because of course "they were just being boys"

when grown men got a look of greed in their eye

and parents were hypervigilant about everything I put on

as a female, how I dressed, behaved, and sat in my chair

determined if I would receive a stigmatizing label

I just wanted to be free, but society said no

only a man can be free, and find his identity without being judged

so, I sat back and looked pretty, while internalizing those messages

and sentenced my potential to a lifetime of misogyny

"The Great Awakening"

I grew up very religious

it is important to realize that this word holds different meaning, context

and relevance to every person.

in my case, this meant attending church weekly

and holding dearly to the values and traditions, like a rule book

growing up, this meant that religion controlled my household

from what we watched on TV, to how we dressed,

and what music we listened to

there was an emphasis on purity and perfection

that was inhumanly possible,

but strived for daily

these values were all centered around sin and repentance,

it was exclusive

we were told that we had to follow the moral code, the holy book or

we would be punished

our lives would go to shambles and we would fall out of touch with the

maker of existence,

we operated under a law that scared us into acting right and shamed us

into hiding our wrongs

constantly falling into the cycle of sinning, shame, defeat, and

inadequacy

only to gain hope through repentance and begin the cycle routinely

week after week, tears falling on the alter like raindrops on a stormy

day

many I knew decided to give up on religion all together

as they watched their leaders use the word

to preach their personal truths and put down others

sharing these truths, I started to question my own beliefs

as I grew up I knew it was time to embark on my own personal journey

I moved away from home and I began to explore many churches

after some time, I stumbled across a place that I connected to

one of the first lessons I learned: Jesus was a man of faith

for the first time I learned what it meant to live by grace

I always thought I had to follow all of the commandments and live this

ideal "holy" life to be considered "saved" or "in right standing with

Christ"

however, I began to see that I was judging my life under the law

I learned that I was eliminating my grace by putting self judgement at

the forefront of my favor that was inherited at the cross

the more I learned, the more I began to understand God and his love

I realized that when he sent his son to die, my imperfections and

mistakes were made righteous

I had access to healing, blessings and worthiness

I had the unearned favor, but, I let the law blind me into thinking I

didn't have the winning

lottery ticket waiting to be cashed in

my identity was complete in Christ and I no longer needed to beg for

forgiveness or strive for perfection

because I was justly right and exactly the person God created me to be

since stumbling across this revelation my life has changed drastically

I no longer fall into that cycle of fear, shame, and regret and inadequacy

I am humble and thankful and focused on my journey and my process

my relationship with Christ is the road map to guide and direct me on

this path

his word is my fulfillment and daily bread

his consistency and loyalty are my comfort

his grace and mercy are my strength and foundation

and his love is my everlasting compassion to shed my personal light into

humanity

"Warm Honey, Sweet Cocoa, Rich Dark Chocolate, and Everything Between"

little brown girls

do not tip your crown, I know that it's heavy

you are strong, your mind more valuable than gold

your skin is soft as silk, your resilience is untouchable

little brown girls

don't let them divide you, you are powerful together

little leaders molding into Queens, Queens building dynasties

don't let them tell you your worth, it is unmeasurable

little brown girls

you come from mothers who refused to give up

that came from mothers who sacrificed and bled to pass down that crown

you deserve to be happy, you deserve to access every gift inside of you

little brown girls

keep singing, dancing, writing, loving

being unapologetically you, crafting the masterpiece you were meant to be

embracing your melanin, embracing your sistas, embracing imperfection

letting the sun, moon, and the rain caress the warmth of your cheeks and the soft wind tousle your beautiful hair

"Unapologetic"

I spent my whole life apologizing

apologizing for being human, for being a woman, for my racial identity

for the discomfort of others, for my existence being offensive

for being too bold, too loud, too confident...

but not anymore

I refuse to be defined, to be classified and boxed into to someone's ever changing expectations

to constantly chase after an unrealistic goal to be considered an accepted ideal

I am beautiful, flawed, wild, uncontrollable, and powerful

I can be sensitive and strong

I can make mistakes and I can totally fail

I am independent, and I understand attachment to others is important

I am smart and ignorant to a lot of things I still don't know about life

I am constantly exploring my world, my environment, myself

I am a work in process constantly evolving and changing

tomorrow I will look at life in a new light, but one thing I will not do is

apologize for being the messy, imperfect, lovable and caring me

I Think I Love You: *Sends Text*

I am not her.

her,

an untainted version of love

a love that you search the depths of earth to find.

her,

a reflection of ideal perfection

the first real bond

a bond stolen as the world welcomed you in

ripping apart the initial connection,

you're back falling into a cold hospital crib

you,

an infant looking into the eyes of nothingness.

of absence.

of neglect.

your voice,

pleading for her comfort

the same way you plead for mine

your lips,

searching for her nipple to pacify

the same way you search for mine,

begging for my embrace, my time, my care.

your ears,

craving for the warmth and familiarity of her voice

the same way you crave for home in my words

your mind,

lost in your past.

in another heartbreak

as I text you back and say,

I am not her.

"The Nuances of Our Six Month Situationship"

I did not want to accept,

the evidence of you disappearing as a present moment

distancing me physically, mentally, and emotionally

leaving my life, while soaking up my energy

my love, my time, my money

now I sit in my dim lit room

farther away from you than I have ever been

staring at these unfinished walls

we began to paint together

a potential masterpiece, paused in time

rum and coke the only company at 2 a.m.

my hands

too tired from pleasing you,

thoughts of regret

running through my mind like a news ticker

my vulnerability exposed

showing the parts of my mind that believed in hope

that saw potential

I jumped

praying for a fair landing,

after every text, phone call, and soft "I love you"

ignoring that little voice in my mind saying

"he won't catch you"

your subconscious truth revealing

the fear of intimacy and closeness

still healing and searching to fill that emptiness she left you with.

the emptiness that I could never fill

as I poured into a reservoir that constantly ran dry,

representing the only cycle of consistency, I would have with you

I should've known that I could never fix you

these psychological circles,

spiraling into the love that I don't deserve

as I accept the things that destroy me

while proving that

I do not deserve better

my candle slowly burns out,

and I seek comfort in the emptiness off your side of the bed

"White Fragility: Sipping on the White Tears until I Blackout"

her voice trembles as she pleads, "I'm sorry"

tears falling beneath those rose-tinted glasses

dripping down those thin white cheeks

her face is searching

searching for comfort in my pain

searching for me to clean it all up

her heart begging for forgiveness

in the blanket of my despair

images of her thin white hands reaching for my crown

a crown passed down for centuries

a container of pain, endurance, resilience, patience

hope

a crown twisted and coiled,

carrying the memories of my ancestors

their struggles, their victories, their wisdom.

she reaches out,

just as her predecessors...

when they reached out and robbed mine

of their dignity, their familial ties, their freedom

two thousand and eighteen years of oppression

constantly minimized and invalidated

her intentions blinding her from the impact

as she mutters that guilty apology

without context to why she is sorry

I've become numb to the apologies

fed up with putting on a mask

my glass running over with these white tears

that I am drinking over and over

as she searches for my empathy

to blot them away

I am running out of wipes to keep avoiding and forgiving

I am tired of the privilege that allows me to continue to experience aggression

the protected whiteness that tells me to suck it up and move on

while I am drowning in these tears

sipping on their shame and regret

"Spiraling"

I could just drive off into nothing

I think I would be okay with that

or... just drink the rest of this cheap barefoot wine

until the room turns into blackness

and the blackness turns into nothingness

this would best depict my mood on a good day

I cannot look in the mirror without seeing this person

the person I said that I would never be

the person I was fighting in time

battling fate

fearful of the angry woman

I have become

terrified of her rage

lips being touched only by select lovers,

whiskey, bourbon, tequila

eyes full of loss

yet searching

for something to be found

I am falling

lost in my mind

plummeting into nowhere

"The Male Gaze"

longing...

desire

telling everything that he plans to do with those hands

his mind, undressing my body

without consent, like he often does

his mouth craving a taste of something

that will never satisfy his whims

"Saving Emotions for Later: Survival Guide for Black Bodies"

as a child, I learned that adults are *always* right

to think otherwise, would get me a whooping

I learned to conform

"don't ask questions and do as you are told, no 'ands' or 'buts'".

this lesson has followed me

constantly reminding me to shut up and do as I am told,

my thoughts don't matter, my voice should be silent, and I don't matter

at least not right now

I don't have time to feel, or think about feeling

I learned that people do not care about how you feel

they care about what you can do

so, I've found distractions and I've grown accustomed to washing down

emotions with strong drinks that burn my chest as the spirit goes down

slowly killing me, but getting me through the day

this trauma and these lessons passed down

nightmares and beatings from the past

whispering to me through the night

"Pick that Cotton!"

tears swell in my eyes, I immediately push them back

I remember the mantra, "I am a strong black woman"

I know pain, but I am not allowed to live in it

I just give and give and give

to a country that kicks me down

strips me bare, and steals the seeds

of the harvest that I produce

giving it a new name and turning it into an acceptable fad

I have become just another body

a nameless face

lost in this mentality

constantly "woke", but emotionally dead

the sun scorches her back

sweat drips from her brow

hands calloused and hard,

fingers tired and cramping,

while she grasps for the cotton

under a Carolina summer Monday

"Venus" FlyTrap

complexity is the essence of your being

and I am intrigued by the challenge

piecing together clues that lead to rabbit holes

of more curiosity

my mind buzzing around the mystery

of your sticky trap--- careful,

but close enough to get you to open

and quick enough to avoid consumption

marveled by your ambition to survive

your patient appetite craving success

sensing opportunity at the cusp of your lips

while savoring the sweetness

in the blood and sweat of a long day

"Sauna"

I am sweating,

this cathartic moisture

coats my golden-brown skin

under the dim glow

of your cheap string lights

as the soft pearly moon pours through the balcony

exposing my vulnerabilities

on the 12 font delicate sheets

cars swish by, floors below unaware of the tension

and I watch the mist fall into the night

while you sink into the mystery of a love letter

my foot taps this fast pace tune of fear

my clammy palms search for comfort in my coat pockets

as I force myself to breathe

in the thickness of silence and uncertainty

blanketing your studio apartment

"Running with Scissors"

running...

defined by an action or movement

leaving behind the past

constantly moving forward

forgiving but never forgetting

running...

accepting the fact that you cannot

change what has happened

but you can act on your situation by continuing to move

scissors...

allowing her wings to cut through the cocoon

and let this beautiful butterfly move

let her be free

free to experience the world

running...

with scissors, involves taking a risk

pushing through the situation

and embracing your freedom

by simply having the courage to move

Share Your Blossoming Journey

As you conclude this book, take some time to write down some experiences that have helped you blossom into the person you are today. After you finish writing, try to embrace those experiences and express gratitude and love towards yourself for making it this far in your journey!

_____

_____

_____

_____

_____

_____

_____

_____

_____

_____

_____

_____

_____

about the writer

Alishia McCullough is a poet and licensed Mental Health therapist from North Carolina. She fell in love with writing at an early age and began writing poetry in early high school. Alishia graduated with a B.A in Psychology and continued her education with an M.S in Counseling. Her passions include topics of empowerment, advancement of women of color, and an appreciation for self-love and compassion. She lives everyday searching for adventure and craving new knowledge and introspection. Her greatest joy in life is serving as a guide for others by helping them cultivate and embody their authentic selves.